# Feed Your Family on $75 per Week

*And eat well!*

Michele C. Moore

Also by Michele Moore:

The Only Menopause Guide You'll Need

together with Caroline deCosta:

Cesarean Section: Understanding and Celebrating Your Baby's Birth

Do You Really Need Surgery?

Dick – a guide to the penis

A Woman's Concise Guide to Common Medical Tests

Midlife, New Life: Pregnancy and Parenting after 35

Just the Facts: Abortion A-Z

*This book is intended to inform and is based in my own experience of feeding a family of four. My early research was done at the side of my maternal grandmother, Rosealba Legault Keib, who fed her family of six through the worst of the Great Depression and World War II. I was very young, but impressionable.*

*I also thank my many friends and colleagues who share m y love of food and obsession with good nutrition. And thanks to my family upon whom I've practiced for more than thirty years.*

*Any factual errors are mine alone; I won't apologize for the philosophical underpinnings.*

Food serves many purposes in our lives; it nourishes our bodies so that we remain healthy and our children develop and grow. It gives us esthetic pleasure as we regard the beauty of a perfect peach or the iridescence of a well-ripened olive. Who among us doesn't have a sense memory of a lemon being cut and its scent filtering through the ambient air? Food also serves a social function, uniting us around a common table, be that of a friend or loved one, or neighboring tables in a restaurant. There is also the pleasure of appreciating a texture on our tongues and in our mouths, like that of a mousse or velvety baked brie. Finally, there is taste. Some may say that this is the finest part of eating food and others that the intricacies of preparing food to bring nutrition and pleasure to others is their personal height of pleasure. Whatever our feelings about food and food preparation, we cannot do without food. In times of economic stress, this can be a challenge. It is for this reason that I've written this book.

In women's magazines, you can find articles that tell you how to cut your weekly marketing cost by collecting and using brand name and store coupons. You are counseled to shop at several grocery stores, finding their bargains and doubling coupons. This undoubtedly can work but is less practical and effective in rural areas, where one may have access to only one or two grocery stores within a reasonable radius. It is also a method that does not have a philosophy of getting more nutritional bang for your buck; mine does.

Gardening can cut your food costs well below $75 per week. From a garden, you can have most of your summer and fall produce or, if you freeze, can and preserve food, you can enjoy the harvest of your garden yearlong.

*I'm not interested in telling you what to have for dinner.*

Michael Pollan

.

# Table of Contents

# Ground Rules

I find that it is helpful to regard shopping within fixed limits as a form of sport; this alleviates the pressure of the economic necessity. As in any form of sport, there are ground rules. These rules help you to achieve your goal by setting some clear boundaries in regard to purchases that jeopardize your ability to feed your family a diet that is high in nutrient quality while needing to stay within a budget of an average of $75/week.

Rule 1. Always shop from a list. This helps to minimize impulse buying. For the same reason, don't shop when you are hungry. If this is unavoidable, chew a stick of gum before going into the grocery store.

Rule 2. Shop once every 7 to 10 days. This ensures that you have fresh produce, dairy products, and fish. It is important that your diet is satisfying, because, as you'll see in a couple paragraphs, you will eat less of some items.

Rule 3. Keep your list handy during the week and add items as soon as you notice you will need them. If you find you lack an ingredient for a recipe in between shopping trips, either defer making that dish until after your next shopping trip or substitute an ingredient that you have on hand. The other night, my son was making a recipe that called for spring onions. We had none, so he substituted half of a yellow onion, which we always have on hand. In other words:

Rule 4. No extra trips to shop! This is easy for those of us who live in rural areas, but if you live in an urban area, you may have the habit of "just running out to pick up xyz."

Rule 5. No bottled water. Invest in a filtering pitcher to filter your tap water. You can then fill reusable water bottles to carry water with you when you go out. Not only will this save you money, it is also more environmentally friendly. In our house, we have some purchased water bottles and we also save any glass tea or juice bottles. They easily go into the dishwasher.

Rule 6. You will save a lot if you switch from paper napkins and towels to reusable cloth ones. I've found in our area, TJMaxx has the best bargains on packages of cloth napkins. If you are going to pay retail price, buy microfiber napkins because they shed a lot of spills and stains. If you like to sew and have time, buy some discounted fabric and make your own. These also make good gifts for family and friends. For rags to wipe up spills, clean surfaces, etc., you can cut up old clothes or you can buy a cheap package of bar wipes or washcloths (again TJMaxx is good, but Bed, Bath 'n Beyond also carries bar wipes in packs of 12) For other paper products, like tissues and toilet paper, I go to a discount food warehouse and save at least 50% on these more necessary products. More on that in chapter 8.

Rule 7. No sodas, pop, soft drink, or whatever you call it, at least not on a routine basis. These are nutritionally empty and should be viewed as rare treats, if part of the diet at all. Since you are no longer buying bottled water, you can't rationalize soda as being cheaper than the bottled water. Water is actually the healthiest beverage for your routine daily ingestion and everything else should be considered a treat to have once in a while.

Rule 8. Milk is not necessary to anyone over 1 year of age, so consumption of milk should not exceed one glass per person per day. Milk is expensive. Talk with your pediatrician about a multiple vitamin supplement for your children to be sure they consume enough Vitamin D . . . or make sure they spend plenty of time playing outside. Other dairy products will be part of your meals and you'll be able to eat plenty of beans and vegetables. Children often fill up on milk or soda instead of eating a healthy variety of foods. There is also scientific evidence that casein, the chief protein in milk, is linked with heart disease, prostate cancer and other ailments.

Rule 9. Buy fruits and vegetables that are in season. They are less expensive, taste better and are healthier for the environment, since those peaches that appear in February have taken a very long plane ride, as has every other out-of-season bit of produce. We all know the luscious taste and scent of a ripe tomato in the summer; compare that with the pale appearance and taste of winter tomatoes. I keep sundried tomatoes in the winter – some that I've dried myself, others purchased. These add more of the real tomato flavor than any winter tomato. My niece pays a premium price for out-of-season blueberries for her toddler; he would enjoy frozen blueberries and gain all the nutritional value from them at a much more affordable price, both for her pocket book and the environment.

Rule 10. All rule systems must have ten rules. This one is simple. Don't buy food just because it is on sale or cheap. If you would not ordinarily eat turnip and have never liked it, chances are that turnip will go to waste. Also, snack foods are not a bargain just because they are on sale. If buying chips at 2 bags for $6 keeps you from buying $6 worth of meat or produce, then those chips have great nutritional cost to you. I find that we are able to buy one snack item each week, although we tend to stick mostly to olives and Triscuits, both of which have nutritional merit. I'm also able to have my one glass of red wine each night and my husband his one beer. More about that later.

# Produce

The produce section is my favorite part of the grocery store. I love the riot of colors, the sharp scents of citrus hovering above the earthiness of potatoes, the smooth satin of bell peppers contrasted with the papery skin of onions. The produce section is a party for the senses.

Vegetables and fruit are essential for your family members' health and fresh produce is far more appealing than frozen or canned. Careful shopping will supply you with a bounty of these fiber and vitamin packed foods. In the summer months, it is not difficult to find affordable fresh produce, either at farm stands, farmers' markets, or in the supermarket. In the winter, it is a bit more challenging, but can still be done. I keep staples like onions and potatoes on hand always and replace them as the home supply gets low. If a store has a special (for example, 5 pounds of potatoes for $1.99) I stock up and store them in a cool dark place. For us, this is a closed paper bag in a cool closet. You can do the same with many other hardy fruits and vegetables, e.g. apples, cabbages (in a cooler in a cold shed), winter squash, turnips, parsnips, carrots, etc.

*Key 1. Buy these hardy, long-keeping vegetables and fruits in the fall and store them at home.* You will pay a fraction of the winter cost of a bushel of potatoes if you buy them in September and store them yourself. The same is true of winter squash and they store very well. Carrots and beets store well in dry sand in a cool dark place.

*Key 2. Berries and soft fruits like peaches and plums are also much cheaper in the summer and can easily be frozen at home.* You can save even more if you pick these fruits yourself. In March, I had a friend visiting from Alaska; she had earlier expressed her nostalgia for strawberry shortcake. I was able to surprise her with shortcake made with local berries that I had frozen in the summer. They tasted like the sun was still shining on them.

*Key3. Some vegetable and fruits are winter staples and are relatively reasonably priced; purchase these.* Examples of these are broccoli crowns (there is more wastage with heads of broccoli unless you save and use the stalks in soups or stews), carrots, turnips, cabbage, kale, beets, cauliflower, Brussels sprouts, apples, some pears, quince (one will add a nice tang to an apple dessert), citrus, pumpkin. A bunch of beets (average price here $2.99/bunch) will give you two vegetable servings: one of greens and one of the roots. Kale is a great bargain all winter long and has a lot of nutrition bang for your buck. I know, kale is an acquired taste, but it can be delicious sautéed in a little oil with garlic and a few pieces of sundried tomato or chopped in soups or stews.

Tomatoes, peppers, asparagus, snow peas, and tropical fruits are deservedly expensive in the winter. Once in a while, your store may have a loss leader on one of these and this would be a special treat. What is a loss leader? This is the advertised special that a grocery store uses as a lure to entice people into the store to shop. Take advantage of these; they enable you to buy more of an item at lesser price or to enjoy an out-of-season treat. For example, in March, I bought green grapes for $1.99 per pound, broccoli for $1.49 per bunch and clementines for $5.99 per crate. These are bargains and we enjoyed them very much, just as we did the 5 pounds of red grapefruit that were featured in February for $4.99. Often, you can find these bargains while preparing your shopping list, by checking the online fliers for your grocery store. You can also sign up for on-line coupons that sometimes help.

Be aware that there is often an environmental trade-off to these out-of-season bargains. I bought asparagus in March for $2.67/lb. Here in NH, asparagus is not available for picking in March. My asparagus was flown from Chile at an environmental cost of $CO_2$. This matters to me. As I mentioned with the berries, you can buy these fragile fruits and veggies in the summer and freeze, can or dry them and preserve that vine-ripened flavor long into winter. I always do this with bell peppers because I love them. I also can and freeze tomatoes so that my family is well-supplied all winter. If you don't want to do this, canned tomato products are usually quite reasonable at discount food stores. Some things, like asparagus and fiddlehead ferns are special treats each spring when they are in season.

*Key 4. Keep staple vegetables on hand.* For me, these are carrots, celery, onions, garlic and potatoes, and cabbage, broccoli or cauliflower in the winter. From these and a few herbs, I can make many delicious meals. For example, one of our family favorites is curried veggies:

1 large onion, chopped     3 cloves of garlic, chopped

½ head of broccoli, separated into florets    2 tbsp oil

3 or 4 carrots cut in coins    1 tsp curry powder

¼ cup water or broth    salt and pepper to taste.

Sauté the onions and garlic in the oil until the onions are translucent. Add the curry, carrots and water and stir. Cook on low heat until the carrots are crisp tender; add the broccoli, salt and pepper. Stir and cook until the broccoli is tender. This is an economical, tasty and very nutritious vegetable dish. With the addition of about 1 pound of chicken, you will have a one-dish meal for 4 – 6 people.

An alternative to both supermarket shopping and home gardening for produce is to join a CSA. What is a CSA? CSA is Community Supported Agriculture and usually refers to an arrangement between a consumer and a local farm, in which the farm agrees to provide a weekly supply of produce to the consumer for an agreed upon fee. Usually the consumer buys one or more "shares" and a single "share" usually provides enough produce for a family of four for one week. Some

20

CSAs provide meat, eggs and dairy products, as well as produce. All CSAs provide a supply season from spring through fall, but it is increasingly common for them to also provide winter produce, from fall through spring. Obviously, this system benefits both the farmer and the consumer. The farmer is assured a market for her products and the consumer is assured a steady supply of fresh produce. It also has the advantage that you, the consumer, can actually inspect the farm from which your food comes. A friend of mine in Barrow, AK belongs to a CSA in the state of Washington and her "share" is flown in weekly at a total cost of $48 per week. She says that it is very adequate for her family of four and that she sometimes has more than they can eat in one week.

I augment my fresh veggies with some frozen ones; as a rule of thumb, I'll use frozen spinach, broccoli or cauliflower if I'm going to be including it in a soup, stew or casserole. I also freeze these from our garden for later usage in soups and stews. Sometimes, I even buy canned beets; they are very cheap (about $0.45 - $0.65 per can) and economical when I want to include them in a meal for many people.

Now that you've stocked up with the week's bounty of produce, you'll need to store it in a way that preserves maximum freshness and therefore, flavor. I've found that green bags actually work. These cost about $10 at regular stores and $3 - $5 at discounters. Although most greens are packaged in plastic bags that help to preserve them, I've found that even they last better if I transfer them to green bags as soon as they are opened.

If your income is very restricted, buy frozen or canned vegetables and fruits. They are usually higher in sodium and sugar so look for low sodium and light syrups labeling, but you will still benefit from them. Plan to spend about 50% of your grocery money on vegetables and fruits.

## The Deli Section

The deli section could rob you of many hard-earned dollars, but there are ways to make it budget friendly.

First of all, do not buy pre-packaged deli meats and cheeses; they are invariably more expensive per pound. Instead, ask the deli personnel if they have any meat and/or cheese ends. These are just what the words imply: the ends of the large pieces of meat and cheese that are sliced or the extra slices that may be more than a customer wants. Surely, you've at least once declined the extra tenth of a pound of ham when you've asked for 1 pound? These days, depending on the particular store, meat and cheese ends range from $1.99 to $3.99 per pound. This is a huge savings over the regular prices. I even sometimes get a slice or two of prosciutto in my meat ends and this is just enough to sauté with a leek and make a frittata. Yum! I like best the stores in which the ends are not pre-packaged. Usually they are a little more expensive when you are able to tell the deli clerk what slices and chunks you want, but the satisfaction is worth it. When I buy an end chunk of ham or turkey, I chop it up and make a salad for sandwiches. I also grate the chunks of cheese for use in cooking or topping other dishes.

Secondly, do not over-buy. These are perishable items and may have been open for a day or two. Buy no more than a week's worth of sandwiches or salads. For my family, with 2 men carrying lunches, this is 1 to 1.5 pounds of lunch meat and about 1 pound of sliced cheese. The cheese lasts longer than a week usually, but this is because I never put more than 1 slice on a sandwich. We don't need more fat.

Other deli items, like prepared macaroni or potato salads, coleslaw, fried chicken, etc. are truly luxury items in that it is so much cheaper to prepare them at home. I rarely even look at these items, because it is easy and inexpensive to make most of them at home. They are not gourmet delicacies.

My family loves olives, pickled garlic and hot peppers, so I do buy these. They cost $7.49 per pound at my supermarket and I usually buy a mixed container of 10 -12 ounces every 2 to 3 weeks. We eat a few with sandwiches and sometimes put a few in a salad. They are our luxury item. Each family needs some simple pleasure like this. In moderation, simple luxuries are affordable.

As a rule of thumb, do not spend more than 25% of your weekly budget on meat and/or fish, unless you are stocking your freezer. Our family has a commitment to eating locally produced food, so I buy our meats from local farmers. Because of this, I buy several times each year, when the particular meat or poultry is available, and freeze the meat. This entails a larger outlay of cash in several chunks each year, but a lower weekly expenditure; the average weekly grocery spending is equal to or less than $75 per week. Our weekly expenditure for meat or fish averages less than $20 per week for 3 to 4 people and occasional guests. We do this because it is important to us to support our local economy, it is more environmentally sustainable to eat local food and we can inspect the farms that produce our food.

You can buy all of your meats, poultry and fish from the supermarket and still maintain a healthy, tasty and varied diet if you shop consciously. If it matters to you whether hormones and other additives are used in your meat and poultry, look for organic or naturally raised and processed meats and chicken. The packaging will state that the product is organic or has been raised in a special manner and contains no hormones or antibiotics. These products are somewhat more expensive than the ordinary meats and chicken, but there are often sales and you can bulk purchase and freeze the sale items. Also, since you are budgeting about 4 ounces of meat, poultry or fish per person, you can easily find a pound of meat for less than $4 - $5 per pound that will feed a family of four. If you need to stretch this, buy cheaper cuts, e.g. chicken thighs instead of breasts, and you can turn a pound of meat into a lovely casserole dish for 6 to 8 people. The cheaper cuts are often tastier if cooked slowly. A four – five pound roasting chicken is always a good buy because it can give you three main meals: on day 1, you have roast chicken; day 2, you have a stir fry or chicken pot pie or chicken salad; day 3, you boil down the bones for a hearty chicken stock for soup. Usually, enough meat adheres to the bones to give good body to the stock. While boiling the bones, tie a bunch of parsley, thyme and perhaps winter savory together and boil it together with the bones. Let the whole mess cool enough that you can reach in and remove the bones and strip off any meat left. To this broth, you can add any variety of vegetables to make a very satisfying soup meal. Either add some potatoes, rice or barley to the soup or serve it with bread. My family loves this meal and it can be as varied as your herb and spice supply and vegetables allow.

Look for cheaper cuts of meat. A Boston butt roast of pork (ask the butcher for equivalents) often costs less than $2 per pound and can make wonderful pulled pork, barbeque or any other braised pork dish. Haven't cooked them before? The Internet is a prolific source of recipes. Beef chuck can make wonderful old-fashioned pot roast and the leftovers make hash or hearty beef soup for another day's meal. You are not condemned to a diet of never-ending grilled or fried ground beef or chicken.

All supermarkets that I've observed advertise weekly specials in meat and poultry. For example, the neighborhood Shaw's is featuring steak tips for $3.99 per pound this week. These specials are usually the best deals for the week. You can consult the weekly specials for your grocery by accessing their online flyer. This saves time and allows you to plan your shopping accordingly.

Fish is expensive but very healthy. Find out which days your supermarket takes delivery of fish, to ensure the freshest purchase possible. All fish is now labeled by country of origin. For the freshest taste, buy fresh, not previously frozen, fish from the USA. If you plan to freeze the fish to use another day, it is best to buy this because fish that has been previously frozen and partially thawed will lose taste on repeated freezing.

Look for the weekly specials. These are often a very good deal and I'll plan a meal around them. For example, when cod is on special for $4.99 per pound, I'll buy a pound of it and make either chowder or a stuffed cod casserole for dinner. Hake is a nice mild white fish that is usually quite inexpensive and cooks nicely. I love it with a Romesco sauce (made with roasted red bell pepper and ground almonds) or with onions and peppers. Your fishmonger will have recipes and can help you try fish that may be new to you. Mussels are almost always inexpensive and can make a good meal or an appetizer for a larger party. Very good deals are often available for salmon and mackerel is usually very affordable. Like salmon, it is a good source of Omega 3 fatty acids. Do not eschew canned tuna, mackerel and salmon. They contain all the healthy attributes of the fresh versions and are a fraction of the price. When I was a child, salmon patties were a common Friday dinner. They were nutritious, healthy and cheap.

Another way to keep your meat and fish budget within bounds is to remember that they are not the only source of protein. It is helpful to the budget to have a bean day and an egg day each week. Beans are good sources of protein and calories and every culture abounds in recipes for beans, ranging from Boston baked beans to chili to feijoada. It is also of interest that peoples who consume mostly vegetable protein have a lower incidence of heart disease, cancer, obesity and diabetes. Eggs are a perfect protein source and are very reasonable, costing around 16 to 20 cents each. Quiches, omelets, frittatas, soufflés, and spoon breads are among the many ways you can feast on the "incredible, edible egg" without breaking the bank.

If you want to host a party for a special occasion, buy your meats ahead and freeze them. This spreads the cost over time and keeps you within budget. Of course, pot lucks are the ideal way to host an inexpensive party.

After reading this, you're probably thinking "I can't do this; I don't have a big freezer and I've never cooked this much." Well, you can; when we started serious economizing we did not have a freezer. Our refrigerator freezer wouldn't hold more than two whole chickens and the garden was producing very well, so we bought a 5 cubic foot chest freezer and have found that this is more than adequate for our family (it involved a little bit of juggling to fit the 16 pound turkey in with 10 chickens, but we did it!) Obviously, we make optimum use of the refrigerator freezer as well. As to cooking, as I've mentioned, the Internet is a great source of recipes and how-to information. Maybe your spouse or children want to pitch in?

Slow cookers are very helpful, especially if you are employed and need to maximize your time as well as your dollars. You can put a soup or stew into the cooker in the evening, turn it on in the morning and come home to the aroma of your succulent meal, ready for you to eat. You can buy a slow cooker for as little as $25. Remember to soak dried beans for several hours, as they cook more slowly in a slow cooker. It's frustrating to dig into a dish of chili only to find the beans are like little pellets.

# Dairy

Milk has become very expensive in the last few years and unfortunately, it is not benefitting the dairy farmer very much. Milk, mother's milk, is the perfect food for babies, but for those of us over one year of age, it is an unnecessary food. We can obtain the nutrients present in milk from other sources and water is better for hydration.

Many of us like milk. . or cream. . or half and half. . in our coffee or tea or on our cereals, but we should understand that this is a taste, not a necessity. Accordingly, when you buy dairy products, budget no more than 1 glass per day for any family member over one year of age. Yes, some will squawk, but they will appreciate their milk even more now that it is a treat. Imagine how much will be saved by those families who have been buying 2 or 3 gallons of milk each week. My aunt had seven children who all liked their milk; her solution to the expense of milk was to mix reconstituted nonfat dried milk with whole milk to double the amount of milk available. It worked for her and may for you. Water is the healthy, inexpensive and available alternative.

Other dairy products are useful in making various casserole meals and providing calcium, protein and other nutrients to a meatless meal. For example, macaroni and cheese relies on the cheese and some milk for its protein; cottage or ricotta cheese make excellent quiches or frittatas and a tablespoon of parmesan cheese will add a lot of flavor to a spoon bread that already has adequate protein from the eggs in it.

Speaking of eggs, although these are not technically dairy products, they are usually in the dairy section of the grocery store. Eggs are sources of complete protein, good fats (if from free run chickens), iron and several vitamins. Egg dishes are an excellent way to have a very inexpensive main dish at least one day per week. These meals can vary from breakfast-at-any-time to soufflés, quiches or strata. Again, you can find many recipes on the Internet, or experiment on your own. Eggs combine with any vegetable, are enhanced by a sprinkle of cheese and can be homemade "fast food."

Yoghurt can be a healthy alternative lunch for a school child; buy a quart of vanilla or plain yoghurt and pack enough in a small lunch container. Flavor the yoghurt by adding a small amount of honey or sugar and a couple tablespoons of fruit. Call it a parfait and your schoolchild will think he has a special treat. Pack some carrot sticks and apple wedges and about 5 Triscuits and it's an inexpensive, nutritious and appealing lunch.

Ice cream is all-American and a staple dessert for many people. Generic brands are now about $2.99 for that box that used to be a half gallon. Buy the generics, limit serving sizes to one scoop and make it a treat. That means that ice cream is served only once or twice a week, depending on how well you've done that week. If you have a taste for premium brands, developed in better economic times, you will need to budget for a much less frequent purchase.

You should be aware that milk protein has been associated in many scientific studies with increased heart disease and cancer, especially prostate cancer. To learn more about this, read The China Study by T. Colin Campbell, PhD.

For some unknown reason, cartons of juice are usually in the dairy section of the grocery. Juice is another item that you can economize; if your family is adamant that they have their juice, limit each person to 4 – 6 ounces per day. Keep in mind that each glass of juice contains the juice of about 4 – 6 fruits, depending on the fruit (and much more for berry juices!). This means that juice is very high in sugar. It is healthier and more economical to serve whole fruits, fresh, frozen or canned.

Also be aware that your juice may be traveling very far to reach you. Until recently, the assumption that your glass of apple juice came from the orchard in your geographic region

37

was a reasonable one. Today, most of your fruit juices are imported, with imports rising 61% between 1993 and 2007. To be more specific, 61% of your apple juice comes from China, 53% of your grape juice from Argentina, and 23% of our orange juice from Brazil. These statistics are from Food and Water Watch. Blends of juices, such as mixed berry, are not required to be labeled with country of origin. This may not matter to you, but it does to me because I want to be sure that the juice I serve my family has met safety and environmental standards. For this reason, I buy only Florida's Natural orange and grapefruit juices because they are the only citrus juices in the supermarket that I can be sure came from the US. I can't imagine buying imported apple juice when I see all the orchards in our New England area. It would be somehow cheating on my relationship with my home. I look carefully at all labels to be sure from where my food comes. It is difficult to impossible to avoid all exposure to food-borne pathogens, but I want to be as careful as I can to not buy foods grown in countries that have no environmental controls or safety

standards or in which agricultural workers are actually or

virtually slaves.

In most grocery stores, the frozen food section is divided into two or three banks of freezers. Along one side will be all the frozen dairy dessert items, like ice cream, sherbet, sorbet and novelty ice cream items. It is a comment on our eating habits that these items, formerly considered great luxuries to be enjoyed on special occasions, now take up an entire side of an aisle. You cannot afford to linger on this side of the frozen foods very long, let alone put many of these items in your cart.

Frozen dairy desserts should be treats that are not consumed with any regularity. When I was a child, going for an ice cream cone was a huge treat. Notice that I said that we went out for this; we could not afford to stock our freezer with ice cream for daily consumption. No one in the fifties and sixties thought that this was a staple of their diet. A child will be healthier if she expects a dish of fruit, fresh, frozen or canned, for her dessert than she will be if served ice cream every day. Our children enjoyed a special treat of 1/3 banana rolled in nuts, with a popsicle stick stuck in the end and then frozen. Eaten frozen, these were as creamy and sweat as ice cream and far healthier. They also liked apple wedges with a thin smear of peanut butter.

Also in the frozen food section are the precooked meals – what we used to call "TV dinners." For the person living and eating alone, these are convenient and possibly cost effective, although many of them are high in fats and sugars. For a family, they are simply a waste of money. The same applies to the meal kits – "just add chicken . . .or beef . . .or". Consider that in these kits, which often are $5 -$6, you are supplied with pasta or rice (ranging from $.65 to $2 for a supply that would feed a crowd), some vegetables, adding up to about one serving of vegetable and a sauce that would cost pennies to make at home with staple ingredients. If it is a "complete meal

– chicken included," the chances are that the amount of chicken in the whole meal would be found in a single half breast, if that. This is no bargain.

I will say that if your family has been drooling for pizza and no one wants to make it from 'scratch', a frozen pizza is more cost effective than a take-out. This could be a treat and fit the budget as long as it is seen as a meal and not a snack.

Frozen waffles can be a time-saving breakfast item and the store brands are often quite reasonable.

Useful and cost-effective items in the frozen food section are the frozen vegetables. These are often less expensive than fresh and supply almost the same nutrient value. Frozen

berries and other fruit can also make good desserts and are definitely cheaper than fresh fruit out-of-season. With all of these items, I am careful to check the country of origin.

When you consider the frozen fruit juices, remember that rationing juice to only 4-6 ounces per person per day is sensible not only from a budget point of view, but also from the health viewpoint. If you do buy frozen juices, the store brands are more affordable and differ little, if any, in quality from the name brands. Again, the country of origin should be listed, unless the juice is a blend of a number of fruits, in which case manufacturers are not required to label the origin.

One mistake that people make when they shop is strolling through the store, aisle by aisle, browsing and noticing things that they didn't previously know that they 'needed.' This is especially insidious if one shops while hungry or without a list. Don't do it! Have your list and only enter the middle aisles for specific items that you need, e.g. detergent, cat food, bread, etc.

When you are shopping the middle aisles, keep in mind the shelving labels that show you the unit prices. These may be expressed as dollars/ounce or dollars/quart or so on, but this is important. This is how you can tell if that big bottle of Tide is really more expensive than the big bottle of Xtra detergent. This may vary from week to week, so note these unit prices each time you shop. For example, I always used to buy Hannaford brand dishwasher detergent until one day I noticed that the price per quart was much less for Sunshine. I'm not sure when Sunshine became cheaper, but it has been true for at least 6 months, and now I check every week. These labels are present for all of the various items, from breads, to soups, to cleaning products, to pet food. Checking them will save you money. If necessary, carry a calculator. I say this because one store may express a unit price as $$/qt and another $$/ounce or gallon and you'll need to convert these values in order to compare them.

Buy sale items – but first, make sure that it really does save you money. I've gone to the store determine to buy Domino brown sugar on sale, only to realize that even at Domino's sale price, the store brand is cheaper. The difference between the two may be less, but there is still a difference. Every one of us probably has one or two items to which we give brand loyalty. For me, that is Hellman's mayonnaise. I simply don't like any other (except Best Food's, which is the same thing), so I wait for good sales on Hellman's and buy 3 or 4 quarts.

Of course, that's only if I haven't been able to buy it at the discount food store (more soon).

Coupons are also helpful, but you still need to do the simple math to make sure that the store brand isn't cheaper. Often it is. There is a trap with coupons: manufacturers don't give them to you as a community service. They are trying to tempt you to buy their product, at a seeming bargain. Remember that a coupon does not save you money if 1) you wouldn't ordinarily buy that item, 2) you don't need the item and it is not a staple, 3) it is not cheaper than a comparable store branded item. Nothing is a bargain if you don't need it.

Many, if not most, of the items in the center aisles of the supermarket are available in discount food stores. If there is a discount food store near you, you will save a lot of money shopping there. It is my policy to never buy paper products, canned goods or cleaning products (except laundry and dish detergent, which I can get cheaper at Hannaford's) at regular price. I found that the prices for detergent were better at Hannaford's by the simple measure of comparing unit prices. Keep that concept in mind when you shop.

You may also have certain needs that necessitate a brand name purchase. For example, I'm allergic to many paper products (yes, they cause me rashes) so I have to stick to the brands that I know are safe. Fortunately, I've been able to find these at my discount food warehouse, but if not, I'd have to fit that regular price purchase into my budget. It is in circumstances like this that coupons are most helpful.

The bakery is the part of the store that I visit least often. It is reserved for treats that I either don't want to make myself or haven't time to do so for a particular occasion.

There are some onion rolls that I have a taste for and will buy sometimes; they are $2.69 per half dozen and I'll buy them only in those weeks when my grocery list is short.

Perhaps for you the taste is for bagels or cookies or donuts; apply my rule of buying only when you have a short grocery list and will spend less than the budgeted $75.

Buying a cake or pie is never cost effective. Even if you don't bake and will rely on mixes, it is so much cheaper to make these items at home. A cake mix will cost you about $1.25 in the grocery store and $0.79 in a discount food store. You will spend about $0.50 for eggs and about $0.25 for oil, for a total expenditure of $2.00 or less to make a cake that will cost you at least $5.00 in the store. Yes, frosting it may add up to another dollar, but you are still ahead.

Remember unit price checking? Do this with the breads and you will find that sometimes the freshly baked bread from the store bakery will be less expensive per pound than the brand named loaves in the middle aisles. This is a sometimes sort of thing and you really need to check it every time you shop.

Usually there is a coffee server in the bakery department. This is a good place to purchase a cup of coffee; it is usually between $1 and $1.25, which makes it competitive with and often cheaper than other coffee sellers. And the coffee is usually good! In fact, it often serves as an advertisement for one of the store's premium brands. (Hannaford's features Green Mountain Coffee) Sometimes, I'm tired or hungry when I shop and I appreciate the little pick-me-up.

## Discount Food Stores

It is only in the last five years of my shopping life that I have become enamored of discount food stores. My husband was way ahead of me in this. You may know these under other names: food warehouses, overstock food stores, sometimes box stores, although these aren't exactly the same. For our purposes, I'm talking about any store that offers deeply discounted foodstuffs.

The store that I frequent is affectionately known as "crash and dent," 'the used food store" and other such nicknames. It is essentially selling overstocked or short-dated non-perishable foods. The store my husband goes to also sells perishables. These are all brand name or store brand items that began their lives on the shelves of some other store and were moved on because they were close to their sell by date (not that they've gone bad, but past the optimum selling date) or are dented cans (yes, in the days when cans had seams, it wasn't good to use a dented can), or crushed boxes or other cosmetic flaws. Let me be clear: these are not tainted goods; they are perfectly edible or usable.

What can you find here? Just about everything that you can find in the middle aisles of the supermarket, but at a fraction of the cost. The drawback? You can't always be sure of finding what you need or want during a specific visit to the store, so you need to keep a running list and visit the store periodically. I never pay full price for Hellman's mayonnaise (remember, I told you it has to be Hellman's for me). At my store, I pay about $2 per quart, so I stock up when they have a good supply. I also pay $0.79 for Ken's or Newman's Own salad dressings, $1.09 for Progresso soups, $1.99 for 5 pounds of sugar, $1.99 for 5 pounds of unbleached flour (and sometimes even for organic whole wheat flour). My family loves Barilla's green and black olive spaghetti sauce and I pay $1.99 for a quart. Because of my problems with some paper products, I need to buy Scott or Charmin toilet paper – I pay $0.45 per roll. Facial tissues are about $1 for a large box of 180 sheets and about $0.79 for a square box of 65 -75 sheets.

Cereals are usually around $2 for a middle sized brand name box (e.g. Cheerios) and often less for store brands. Grains, like rice, oats and pasta, are significantly less expensive than in the grocery store. In fact, pasta (brand names) may often be sold at 2/$1.00 or even 3/$1.00

Oils, such as extra virgin olive oil and canola oil are also bargains here. Smart Balance oil blend is $1.79 for 48 ounces and a quart of extra virgin Spanish olive oil is $2.99.

Junk food isn't such a bargain. Liter bottle of soda are $0.99. It is a bargain if you are particular about a brand name, but if you are simply looking for cheap soda, Adirondack soda in the regular grocery store is the best buy. Chips, pretzels and such snacks are not usually any cheaper in some discount food stores than they are in the supermarket. This is not always true, so you'll have to be aware of prices when you shop. For example, in the store my husband goes to, there may be big bags of chips selling at 3/$1.00. You can't count on it, but it has happened.

Household cleaning products are another category that may or may not be less expensive than the supermarket. The large tub of OxyClean is $7.98 in my supermarket and $4.99 in my discount food store. Still expensive, but much less so. On the other hand, I've not found a dishwasher detergent that is cheaper than Sunlight in Hannaford's. You have to look and compare.

Some cosmetic items can be found, as well. I like a particular shampoo that costs $7.99 at the supermarket. When they have it at the discount food store, I snatch it up at $2.99. I allow myself this little luxury because I only use about 2 bottles per year.

Canned and bottled juices are also much less at the discount store. A forty-eight ounce bottle of juice usually costs $1.99. This includes all the brands, including, but not limited to, Ocean Spray, Juicy Juice, Apple and Eve, Knudsen's, V-8, etc.

When fresh produce is available it is often slightly bruised, a little brown at the edges or slightly limp. It requires careful selection, but my husband has brought home beautiful organic cauliflowers for a quarter, bags of organic spinach with no blemishes at all, and bags of organic apples at $0.25 per pound. It is hard to beat these bargains.

He also loves buying a case of granola for $2.00 and a case of yoghurt for $3.00. Yes, a case! 12 boxes or cartons.

Obviously, I can't list all of the bargains that are to be found, and they do vary from location to location, but you see that shopping in these stores can save you a lot of money.

Some of the "box stores" have impressed me less because I'm a compulsive label reader and I don't want to eat a lot of food from China. The lack of health standards and environmental controls overrides my enthusiasm for a bargain.

# End Word

I hope that you have gained some ideas and skills that will help you in your quest to feed your family in a healthy and economical way. Although I have budgeted for $75 per week, you can adjust this to your own budget and it will work equally well. The $75 is an average figure; some weeks I spend only $56 and others, it may be $83.

Remember that nothing is cheap or a bargain if you don't really need it or if it isn't of high nutritional value. The old saying "an apple a day keeps the doctor away" has truth in it and the message is that we need to feed ourselves in a wholesome way to maintain health.

Made in the USA